COURSE WORKBOOK

PUT THAT Shhhh... IN A BOOK

HOW TO TELL YOUR STORY
WITHOUT TELLING YOUR STUDENT'S BUSINESS

COPYRIGHT © 2021 MASK OFF PUBLISHING, L.L.C.

All rights reserved. No part of this workbook can be reproduced, distributed, transmitted, or used in any manner without written permission of the copyright owner except for the use of quotations in a book review.

804 Main Street, Ste. A Baton Rouge, LA 70769
bookinfo@maskoffpublishing.com
To get your book published go to: www.maskoffpublishing.com

A NOTE FROM THE AUTHOR
WELCOME, MY BEAUTIFUL PEOPLE

Put That Shhhh In A Book: How To Tell Your Story Without Ever Telling Your Business, was born through my stories that became books. I was delivered, healed, learned forgiveness, patience, and perfected my love while writing books that did not tell my business but provided messages that would help others have the same results or better.

Telling stories, creating helpful material, and inspiring others allowed me to rewrite my narrative. I realized that other people's lives could change if they rewrite their narratives while keeping their business private.

In helping others through coaching, I decided to offer a course that would reach more people and cause a more significant impact. Writing is good for our life but best for the lives of others.

After taking this course, *Put That Shhhh In A Book,* you will publish a book from outline to online successfully and inspire others with your message of change.

This supplemental workbook will not take the online course's place but will provide support throughout the process, assist you in taking notes effectively, and guide you while taking action.

Kristie F. Gauthreaux

Kristie F. Gauthreaux
Founder of Mask Off Publishing

WRITE NOW

THE **WRITE** METHOD

INSTRUCTIONS: Use the checklist to keep track of your workbook journey. Once you have completed a part of the journey, place a ✓ in the box.

READ INTRODUCTION

- [ ] **W** WHY
- [ ] **R** RIGHT AUDIENCE
- [ ] **I** INFORM FROM PLATFORM
- [ ] **T** TALK IT OR TYPE IT
- [ ] **E** EDIT/SELF EDIT/PEER EDIT/PROFESSIONAL EDIT

- [ ] **N** NAME IT & FRAME IT
- [ ] **O** OWN IT
- [ ] **W** WORK IT & WIN IT

READ CONCLUSION

©2020 MASK OFF PUBLISHING L.L.C.

INTRODUCTION

INTRODUCTION

YOU'RE IN THE RIGHT PLACE FOR THE RELEASE YOU NEED

- Do you have repeated disturbing memories, thoughts, or images?
- Do you have bad dreams?
- Do you live in fear of someone finding out what happened?
- Do you get upset when something or someone reminds you of the event?
- Do you notice physical changes (heartbeat accelerates or heavy breathing) when you think or talk about the event?
- Do you avoid talking about the event or people involved?
- Do you feel emotionally numb?

If you answered "Yes", you need to Put That Shhhh! In A Book, (PTSB)
PTSB will help you gain control of your secret thoughts, organize them in a way that allows you to live more freely, and rewrite your shoulda, woulda, coulda!

Keeping a secret is the culprit that robs you of your freedom. Some secrets haunt you for life, prevent you from sleeping, give you anxiety, or even drive you into depression. Secrets take away your freedom, and when you live chained to an event that can never be shared; you take a dose of fear every day. You live with the worry of someone finding out what happened and what they think of you because of it.

Consider the life changing coping methods, prayers prayed, resources, and other things you used that can free others. Staying silent about attacks, trauma, violence, or even neglect is intentionally holding back the freedom for someone else. You can liberate yourself and others by telling your story while never telling your business....

- There is a way to tell your story without telling your business!
- There is a way to rewrite your narrative and gain strength!
- There is a way to escape and liberate others!

SECTION ONE
workbook

WHY

WHY IS YOUR MESSAGE IMPORTANT?

YOUR WHY

Your why will come through a strong desire to help others. You can find it in the conversations that you have with yourself and others. It is usually joined with the words, "If I had known, I could have, I should have, I would have, I will never do that, I know better next time," and those alike. In those talks, you identify the weaknesses, the strengths, the sneaky beginnings, and the red flags. You know what decision you made to overcome or the choices you should make but do not yet have the courage.

Your why is the fuel that will propel you into the deliverance you deserve, the freedom you are seeking, or onto the platform where you speak wisdom to those who need to be where you are. Your why is easy to find if you switch your focus from where you are to where others can be. It is just that simple. See the life-changing results for others, and ask yourself how did they get there. Once you have done this, you will be able to craft a message from your story that will help you rewrite your narrative, keep your business private, and release people who are bound.

As you move into the next pages, use your real emotions, the hurt and pain, the excitement, and victorious passions to help format your why. By the end of this section, you will know what message you want to deliver to your audience and why.

W-WHY

- IDENTIFY YOUR WHY
- EXPLAIN YOUR DESIRE TO HELP OTHERS
- HOW YOU WILL DO SO

HOW LONG HAVE YOU KEPT QUIET

- almost my entire life
- half my life
- 10 years or less

WHAT HAVE YOU DONE TO COPE

- prayer
- counseling
- self development or other

HOW DO YOU WANT OTHERS TO FEEL:

- Safe
- Grateful
- Balanced
- Free
- Loved
- Happy
- Other:

STEP 1: IDENTIFY THE THEME, SUBJECT, OR ISSUE THAT YOU WANT TO ADDRESS

STEP 2: WHAT FREEDOM STEPS WOULD YOU RECOMMEND AND WHY

STEP 3: USE TWO FEELINGS TO CREATE A SENTENCE THAT EXPLAINS WHY YOU WANT OTHERS TO FEEL THAT WAY

- DESCRIBE WHAT THOUGHTS KEPT YOU BOUND AND MAY BE KEEPING YOUR AUDIENCE BOUND
- PROVIDE FREEING THOUGHTS OR WORDS

NEGATIVE THOUGHT:

POSITIVE AFFIRMATION:

NEGATIVE THOUGHT:

POSITIVE AFFIRMATION:

NEGATIVE THOUGHT:

POSITIVE AFFIRMATION:

NEGATIVE THOUGHT:

POSITIVE AFFIRMATION:

- SET GOALS AND CREATE A VISION YOU WANT YOUR AUDIENCE TO HAVE
- IDENTIFY BARRIERS
- PROVIDE SOME ACTION STEPS

QUESTION #1: What are your goals and vision for your audience?

QUESTION #2: What obstacles might they face?

QUESTION #3: What more could they do to reach their goals?

Quotes For Success

Do you have an original quote or quotes? Create four original quotes for this section of your book.

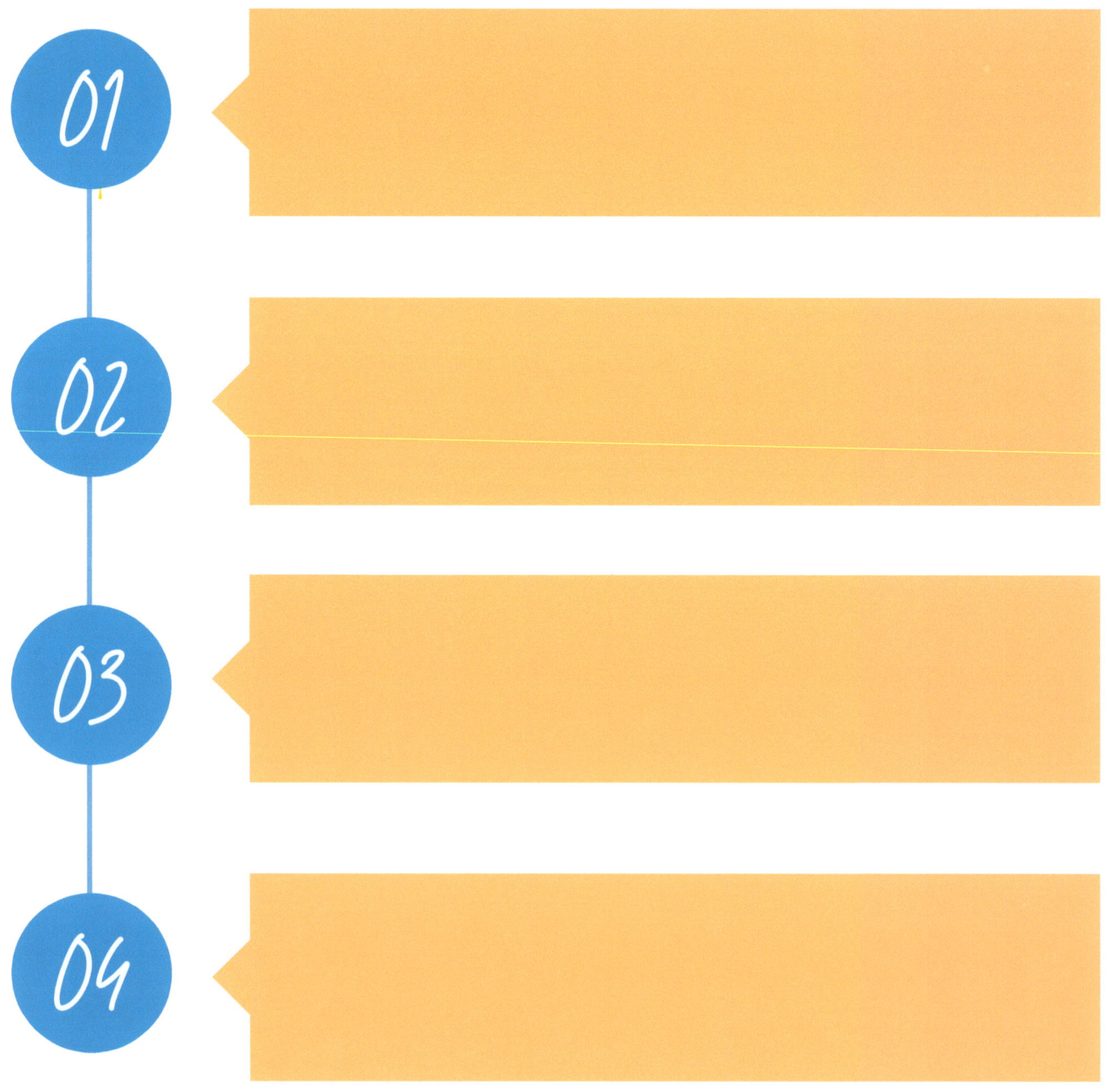

Quotes For Success

Quotes For Success

WRITE NOW

WRITE NOW

WRITE NOW

WRITE NOW

SECTION TWO
workbook

RIGHT AUDIENCE

WHO IS YOUR RIGHT AUDIENCE?

RIGHT AUDIENCE|RIGHT PERSON

You are the right person for this assignment and choosing the right audience will come easy. Your audience relates to your story in some way, and only you can identify who they are. You have to choose whom you want to speak to directly. For example, if you were writing a message about domestic violence, would you write to the victim, the victim's parents, or even more specific to the children? Identify the person who needs communicating with the most.

Whose problem do you want to help solve? Some authors like to say their message is for everyone. Unfortunately, that is not true unless you are talking about a situation that applies to everyone. See the person reading your book and understand they are human, just like you. Do not choose your audience based on potential cash flow; choose according to whom you can help. Your target audience can also include those who work with, teach, nurture, or support the right person or audience.

As you move through the next pages, you will answer the following questions:
- What is the problem they face?
- How old are they?
- What gender are they?
- What is their religion, belief, or ethnicity?
- Where would they shop to purchase your book?

By the end of this section, you will identify the right audience for your message.

R-RIGHT AUDIENCE

- ADDRESS THE CHALLENGE THEY FACE
- DESCRIBE THEM AS IF THEY ARE AS YOU WERE
- GIVE THEM THE WISDOM YOU USED OR SHOULD HAVE USED

QUESTION #1: What challenge is your audience struggling with at the moment?

QUESTION #2: Describe the right person or audience? How old are they? What is their ethnicity? Are they male or female? What is their religion and how does it apply or not in this situation?

INSTRUCTIONS: Imagine your perfect morning routine was just interrupted by a phone call. On the call they explain that they're in a situation similar to yours. They want your advice. In one, 7 sentence paragraph, give them wisdom or a new way of seeing things.

QUESTION #1: EXPLAIN HOW ADDRESSING THE CHALLENGE MADE YOU FEEL FREE OR CAPTIVE?

QUESTION #2: WHAT'S STANDING IN YOUR WAY?

QUESTION #3: EXPLAIN HOW COMFORTABLE YOU ARE WITH HELPING THE PERSON/PEOPLE YOU DESCRIBED?

QUESTION #4: WHAT ARE YOUR NEXT STEPS?

QUESTION #5: WHAT WAS THE MOST IMPORTANT PART OF YOUR JOURNEY? CIRCLE WHAT YOU BELIEVE IS THE KEYWORD!

✓ EXERCISE #1: MEDITATION - POSITIVE AFFIRMATIONS

BEFORE I THOUGHT...

NOW I THINK AND SAY...

MY THOUGHTS, INTUITIONS, REALIZATIONS...

✓ EXERCISE #2: BREATHING TECHNIQUES

BEFORE I FELT...

NOW I FEEL...

MY THOUGHTS, INTUITIONS, REALIZATIONS...

✓ EXERCISE #2: VISUALIZE

BEFORE I SAW...

NOW I SEE...

MY THOUGHTS, INTUITIONS, REALIZATIONS...

QUESTIONS FOR YOUR AUDIENCE

WHAT QUESTIONS WILL YOU ASK THEM?
WHAT QUESTIONS WOULD THEY ASK YOU?

#1

#2

#3

WRITE NOW

WRITE NOW

WRITE NOW

WRITE NOW

SECTION THREE
workbook

INFORM THROUGH PLATFORM

CHOOSE THE RIGHT BOOK FORMAT

INFORM THROUGH PLATFORM

Now that you have a well-crafted message and a visual of who your audience is, decide what platform or type of book, you want to use for delivery. Keep in mind; you are not writing an autobiography, that delivery will require you to tell your secrets, which is not the objective for this course. Ask yourself these questions to help you decide:

- What books or videos did I watch or listen to that motivated or helped to transform my life?
- Did I pray, meditate, visualize, or write for comfort and relief?
- Did I seek counseling, family help, or a friend's ear, and did it help?
- What things did I find gratitude in, while I went through the situation?
- Am I still attached or bound, and am I using this opportunity to rewrite my narrative?
- Have I forgave all who need forgiveness, and have I forgiven myself?
- Did I use any form of physical fitness to help relieve stress and provide mental comfort?
- Would I use any of my above answers as a guide to help someone else?

Once you have these questions answered, review your responses, and match them with the platforms you believe will deliver it best.

INFORM THROUGH PLATFORM

CHOOSE THE RIGHT BOOK FORMAT

LIST OF PLATFORMS

Choose which one you believe will carry the message effectively.

1. **JOURNAL** - A journal allows the audience to write their truths, emotions, hopes, intentions, or affirmations.
2. **DEVOTIONAL** - A devotional can feed wisdom and hope to the audience. The devotional will minister to them in quotes, scriptures, affirmations, or even short words of wisdom.
3. **PLANNER** - A planner can provide both the devotion and journal aspects while presenting intentional methods to provide the audience some relief.
4. **HOW-TO/SELF HELP** - A step-by-step guide will give the audience practical or spiritual steps to help them out or gain relief.
5. **SHORT STORIES/SERIES** - A short story is a platform for a new narrative, anonymous characters, and creativity that flirts with reality.
6. **COLORING BOOK** - A coloring book is a platform that can contain any of the above platforms.
7. **CHILDREN'S BOOK** - A children's book will display the message to a younger crowd and spark their imagination where all change originates.
8. **GRAPHIC NOVEL** - A graphic novel will tell the story, relay the message through characters and settings, and show actions both the good and the bad. It also provides an excellent platform for villains and heroes.
9. **MAGAZINE** - A magazine is a platform made to cover many aspects of the message using columns and pictures from various resources.

I-INFORM THROUGH PLATFORM

- REVIEW YOUR RESPONSES
- READ THROUGH THE PLATFORMS
- APPLY THE RESPONSE THAT MATCHES THE PLATFORM EXPLAIN WHY

JOURNAL:

DEVOTIONAL:

PLANNER

HOW-TO/SELF-HELP:

COLORING BOOK:

I-INFORM THROUGH PLATFORM

- REVIEW YOUR RESPONSES
- READ THROUGH THE PLATFORMS
- APPLY THE RESPONSE THAT MATCHES THE PLATFORM EXPLAIN WHY

CHILDREN'S BOOK:

GRAPHIC NOVEL:

MAGAZINE:

ROMANCE NOVEL:

OTHER: THINK OF YOUR OWN

- COMPLETE EACH EXERCISE TO HELP YOU DEVELOP A SOLID PLATFORM

✓ EXERCISE #1 WRITE TO YOUR COWORKER

| I AM HELPING OTHERS... | MY BOOK IS A...IT HELPS... |

✓ EXERCISE #2: WRITE TO YOUR CLOSEST FRIEND

| I AM HELPING OTHERS... | MY BOOK IS A...IT HELPS... |

✓ EXERCISE #3: WRITE TO YOUR AUDIENCE

| I AM HELPING YOU... | MY BOOK WILL HELP YOU... |

Pretend you are talking to each person or group of people. Use the sentences starters to help you talk about your mission and the purpose of your book.

STEPS YOU WILL TAKE

Instructions: Write down the steps you will take to form and solidify your foundation.

STEPS YOU WILL TAKE

Instructions: Write down the steps you will take to form and solidify your foundation.

WRITE NOW

WRITE NOW

WRITE NOW

WRITE NOW

SECTION FOUR
workbook

TALK IT OR TYPE IT

MANUSCRIPT MUST BE DONE

MANUSCRIPT

Now that you have a crafted message and know who your target audience is, you must prepare that sacred manuscript. You will soon begin to outline, free write, organize, and build your book's foundation. Your platform must have a solid foundation to deliver your story to the right people effectively.

First, decide if you will talk out your designs or type them. You have complete control of your book project unless you choose to have someone else do it for you. Yes, that is possible, and people do it every day. Writers are looking for hire and will write your manuscript for you. Those writers are called ghostwriters.

Ghostwriters:

Ghostwriters write various works, at a cost, but do not take the credit for it. There are resource sites that can help you find one who can deliver according to your standards and expectations. Here are some necessary steps you should take if you decide to take the ghostwriting journey.

- Design a plan that creates an easy path for the writer to understand and follow to meet your expectations.
- Do the research! Many sites are offering ghostwriting services. Read the reviews of the site or ghostwriter you choose. Conduct a more in-depth dig, go past the website's surface, find blogs and reviews to receive additional insight.
- Look for previous works completed by the ghostwriter. Ensure their expertise align with your ideas and genre. Choose a writer with experience, quality work, and great reviews.
- Answer the question, will this ghostwriter understand and effectively capture my style? You and the ghostwriter must communicate expectations, strategies, methods, and other mechanics for your project. It would be best to give clear and concise objectives, express yourself with integrity, and allow the ghostwriter to learn your voice.
- Remember, choose a ghostwriter for the quality of work, not their fees. Just because it will save you money does not mean you will get the completed work in the way you expect it and deserve it.

TALK IT OR TYPE IT

MANUSCRIPT MUST BE DONE

MANUSCRIPT

Do It Yourself:

Write a manuscript that will introduce your message and transform the lives of the audience. Use these next seven steps to complete your manuscript.

- Commit to your success. You have a desire to help others through your message, and you have the tools. Therefore, you no longer own procrastination and failure. You can do this and will do this if you DO THIS! COMMIT!

- Start writing! Open a document on your computer or a document in Google docs on your phone and start free-writing. Free-writing will give you the mental and fine motor exercise you need to start this writing journey. It doesn't matter if you are writing the same event repeatedly, you must type something every day. If you don't know what to type, type your message to your audience and keep going with whatever comes to mind. Now IS NOT the time to format, check grammar, rewrite, or be technical. JUST TYPE!

- TAKE YOURSELF SERIOUS! Every day you should support your book by adding to it. Remember your book is a platform to offer change to the reader. Therefore, you must remain consistent in the building process; a weak platform will not support your message.

- Begin the organization process after you have built up your writing stamina. Start by creating an outline or graphic organizer. An outline and graphic organizer will assist you with putting the chapter titles and information in a sequence that would make it easy to fill in the details. With an outline, you can list the order in which you want to write. Using a graphic organizer will allow you to draw, label, and be more creative with your book project. There are also other methods to help you get organized.

TALK IT OR TYPE IT

MANUSCRIPT MUST BE DONE

MANUSCRIPT

- Do your research, do your digging, use your resources, conduct interviews, or use other methods to find the essential facts or stories to highlight in your book. All books require some form of inquiry, whether to find factual evidence, quotes, scriptures, or similar stories to get fresh ideas. There is information in other places that will bring light to your project.

- Fill in the details. Once you have the framework in place, place the details in their proper place. You can do this by using your outline as a guide. Move through your manuscript chapter by chapter. Understand you are now working on the first draft, and it is okay to make mistakes. In writing the first draft, you will write much of what you do not want, so write and remove the errors later.

- Finally, read what you have two times without any editing. Go back in the third time to rephrase, rewrite, move characters, add steps, take things away, add more details, and make other big moves. This will ensure that you are confident in the message, platform choice, and delivery. You can strengthen the writing as you go into the editing process.

T-TALK IT OR TYPE IT

- Free-write and rewrite to get the words flowing
- Write out your feelings
- Organize your information

INSTRUCTIONS: Use this page to free-write your old story and rewrite your narrative. If you are still in the story and are not writing in deliverance, write the narrative you desire to have.

OLD STORY | NEW STORY

- Free-write and rewrite to get the words flowing
- Write out your feelings
- Organize your information

INSTRUCTIONS: Use this page to freely rewrite your narrative or the narrative of someone you know.

Remember, you are the author of a new story or the teacher of new ways.

_____
_____
_____
_____
_____
_____
_____
_____
_____
_____
_____
_____
_____
_____
_____
_____
_____

- Free-write and rewrite to get the words flowing
- Write out your feelings
- Organize your information

INSTRUCTIONS: Continue to use this page to freely rewrite your narrative or the narrative of someone you know.

_____
_____
_____
_____
_____
_____
_____
_____
_____
_____
_____
_____
_____
_____
_____
_____

INSTRUCTIONS: Use this page to write out your feelings towards this book project. How did you feel before you started, and how do you think now that you have?

BEFORE

BEFORE

INSTRUCTIONS: Use this page to write out your feelings towards this book project. How did you feel before you started, and how do you think now that you have?

T-TALK IT OR TYPE IT

INSTRUCTIONS: Use these pages to organize your chapters, characters, events, categories, or steps. In the center, choose the two most important topics and use the outer hexagons for details.

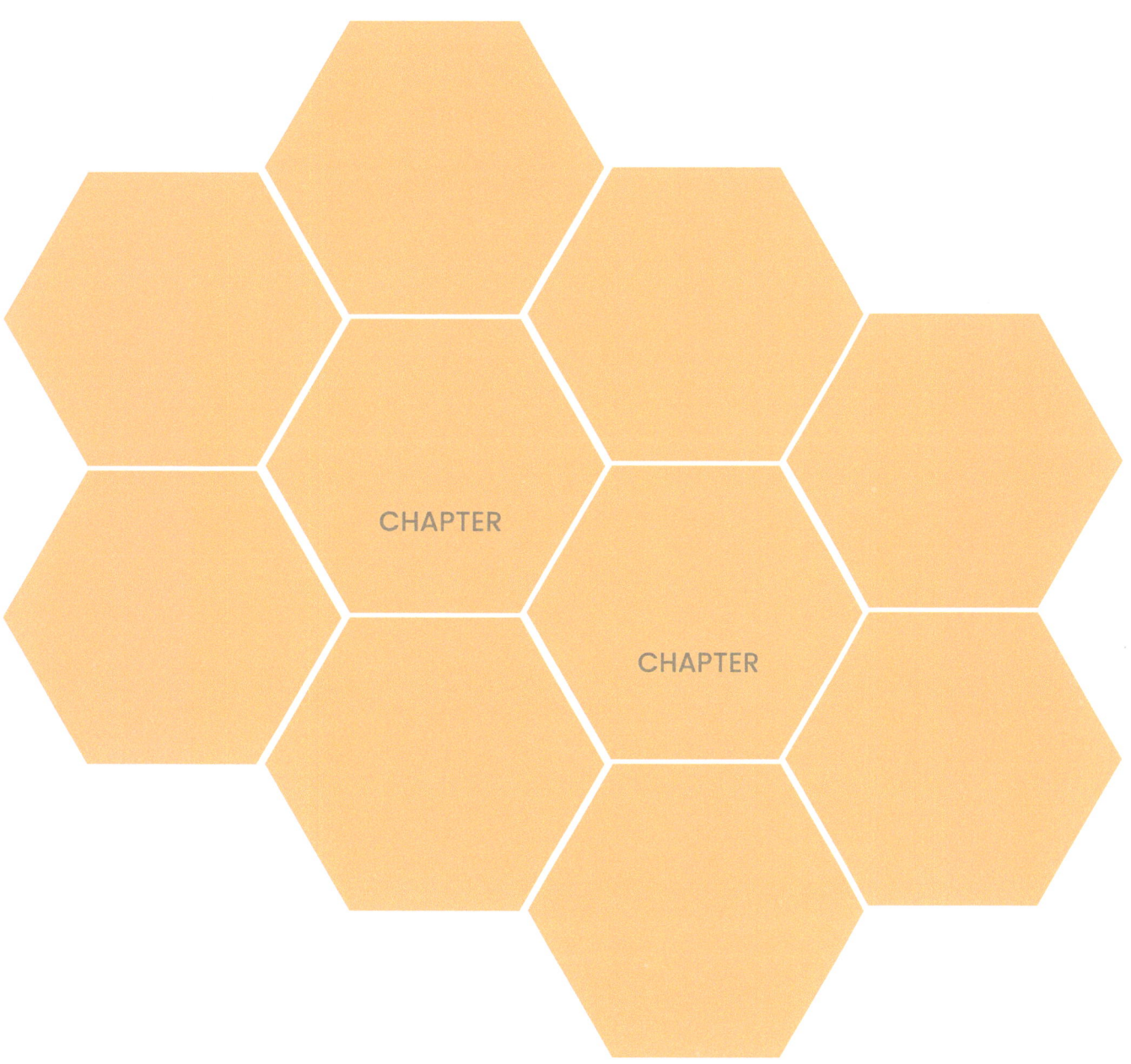

*USE THE HEXAGONS TO ORGANIZE INFORMATION..

INSTRUCTIONS: Use these pages to organize your chapters, characters, events, categories, or steps. In the center, choose the two most important topics and use the outer hexagons for details.

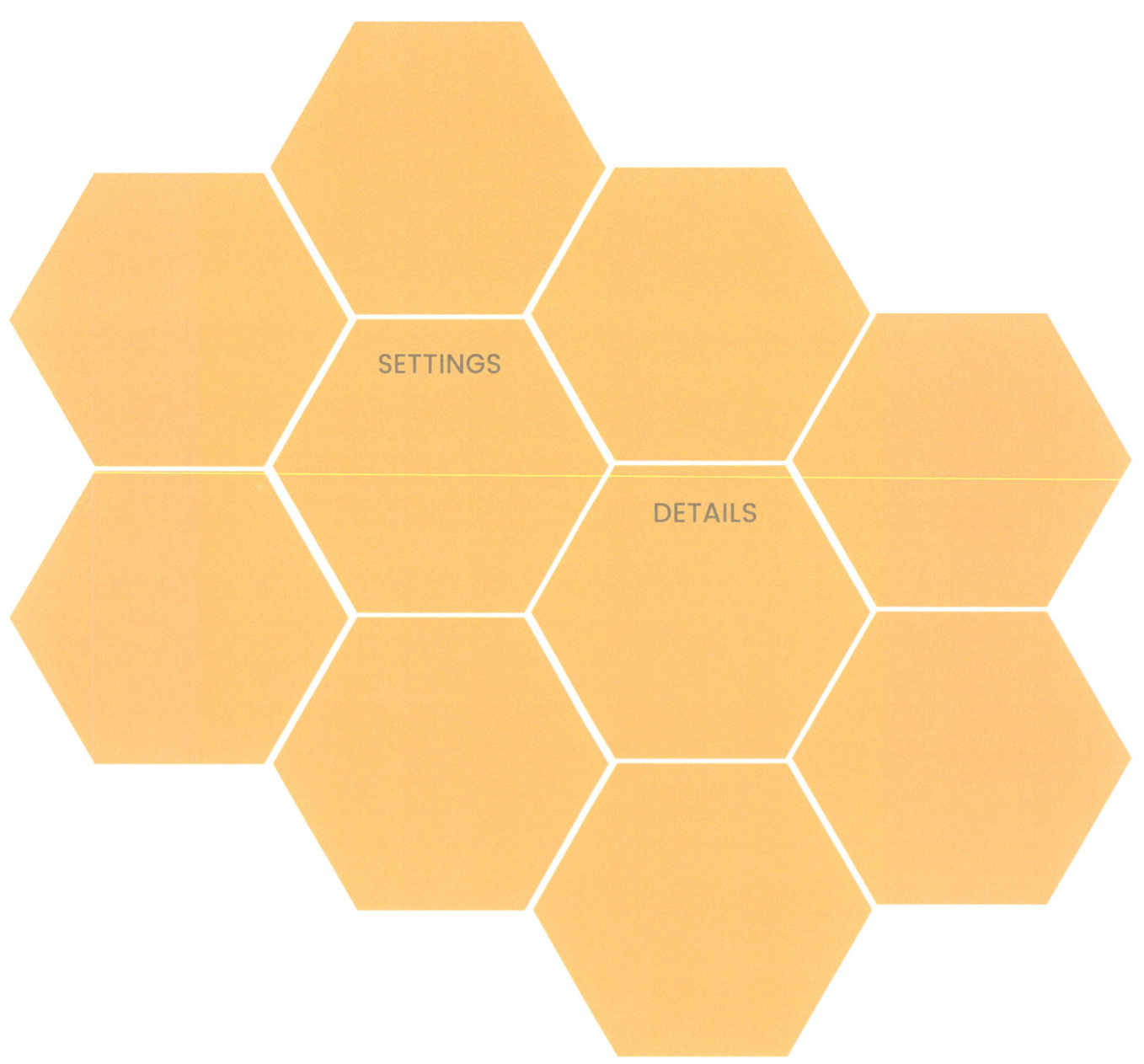

*USE THE HEXAGONS TO ORGANIZE INFORMATION..

INSTRUCTIONS: Use these pages to organize your chapters, characters, events, categories, or steps. In the center, choose the two most important topics and use the outer hexagons for details.

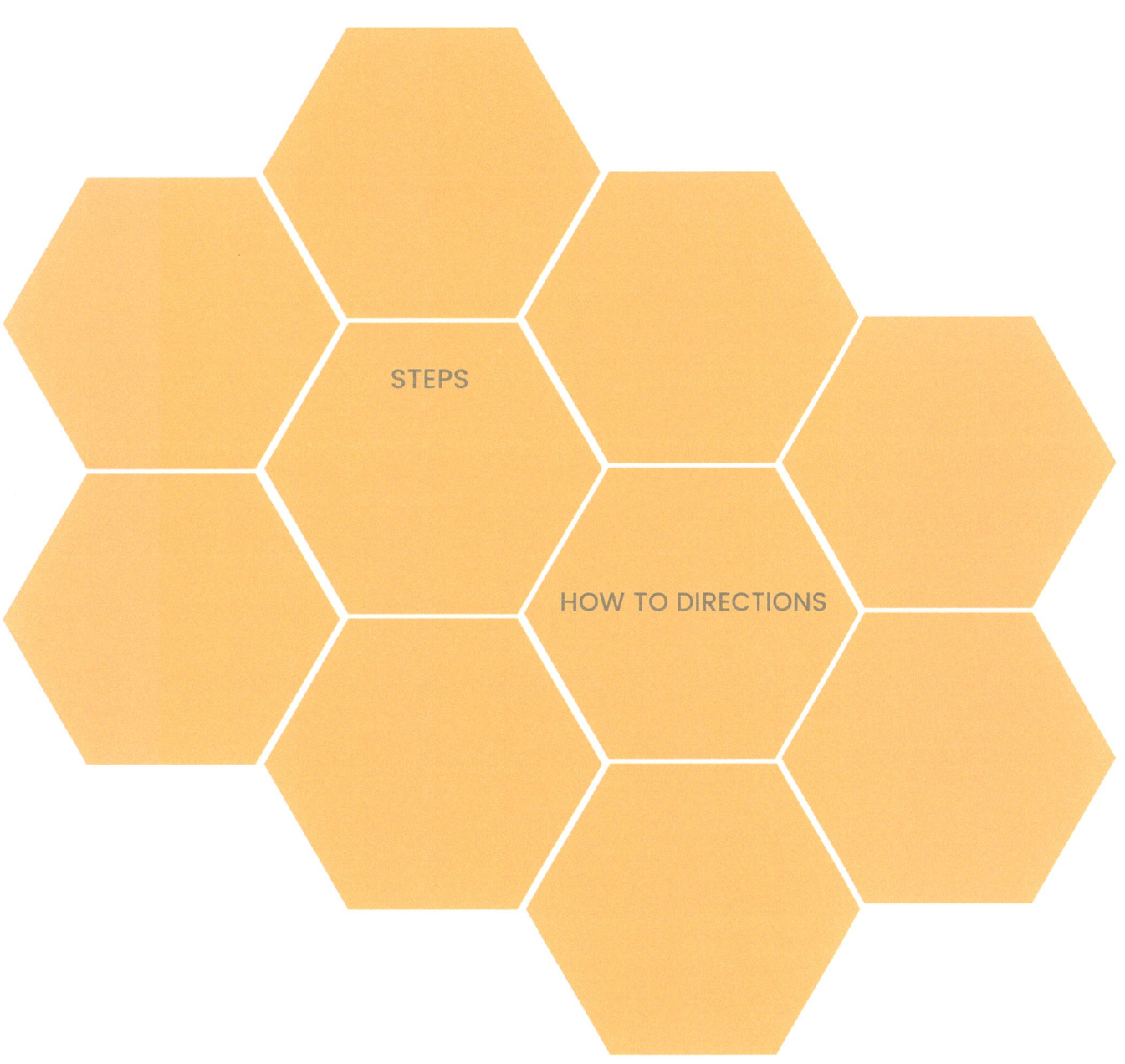

*USE THE HEXAGONS TO ORGANIZE INFORMATION..

INSTRUCTIONS: Use these pages to organize your chapters, characters, events, categories, or steps. In the center, choose the two most important topics and use the outer hexagons for details.

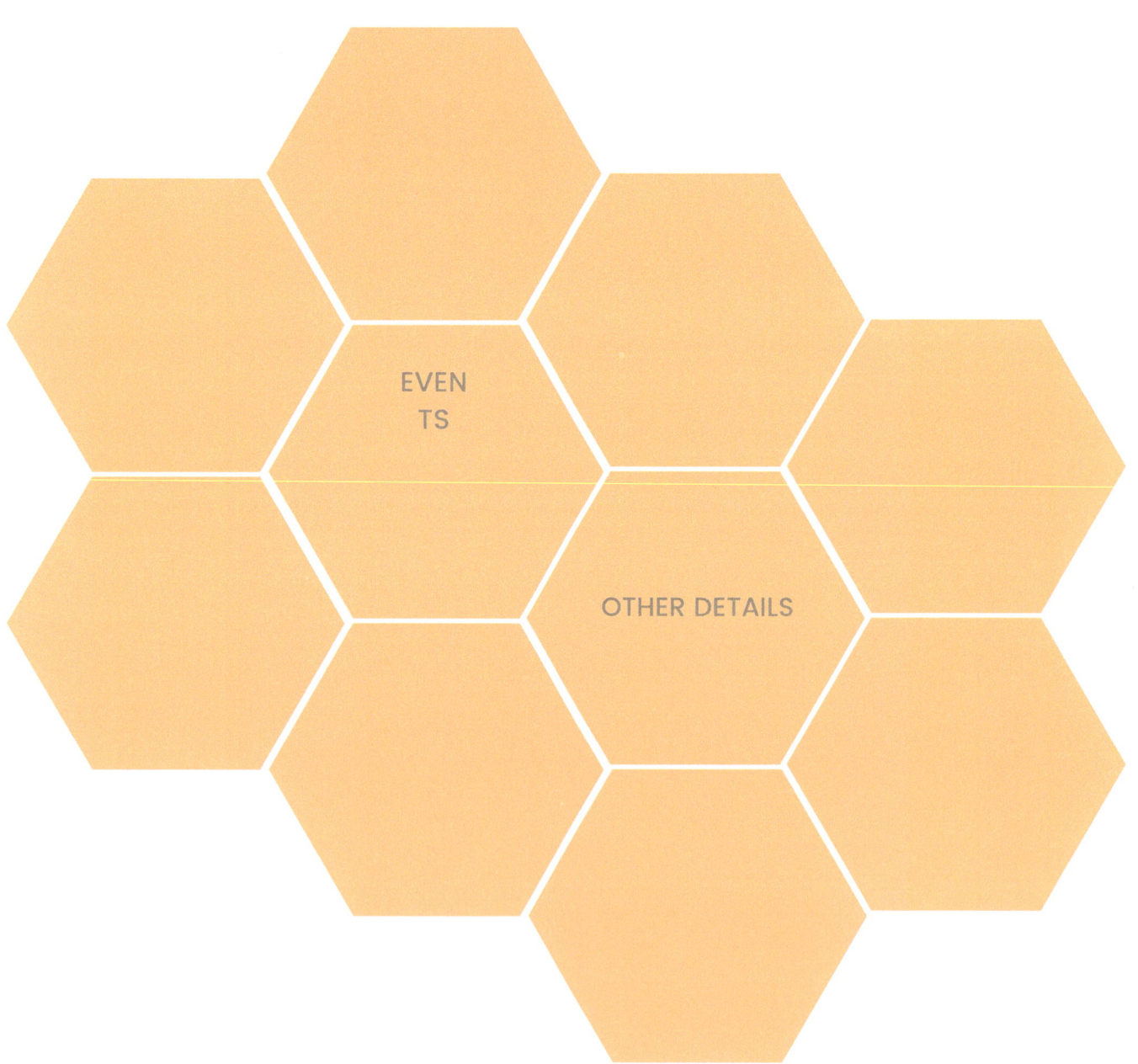

*USE THE HEXAGONS TO ORGANIZE INFORMATION..

WRITE NOW

WRITE NOW

WRITE NOW

WRITE NOW

SECTION FIVE
workbook

EDITS

SELF EDIT, PEER EDIT, PROFESSIONAL EDIT

Self Edit:

Self-editing begins on the fourth read-through. Self-editing is the first layer of refinement; take some time to read the manuscript as a new reader. Here are a few steps to take to ensure a thorough self-edit.

- Read and edit the manuscript. If it is typed in MS Word, turn on track changes, leave comments, and use the tools to check for errors. If did in Google Docs, add comments, turn on spelling and grammar check, and review suggested edits. In doing these things, documented corrections will be visible to the peer editor or a beta reader. This will allow them to agree with changes, respond to comments, create comments and changes, or make suggestions.
- Download an editing software or app. There are free versions that will aid in basic editing. However, if possible, sign up for the premium service and use it before sending the manuscript to the peer editor or beta reader.
- If the book will be a printed version, print it out, and read it. Sometimes reading the manuscript page by page will help determine the flow from section to section. Use sticky notes to document changes, add notes, or move parts around.
- Search out peer editors to do the next round of edits. Ask friends, family, spouse, or someone who is the ideal reader to provide editing feedback. Give concise instructions, ask that they be honest, and prepare to receive their comments, changes, and suggestions.

Peer Edit:

This is necessary, but It can also be biased if done by a close family member or friend. When or if possible, allow one to two distant friends, family members, or strangers to read and review the manuscript.

Professional Edit:

Professional editing is the most important step in the book writing process. DO NOT SKIP professional editing. The only exception for this process is if you are publishing a journal or planner that includes a very small amount of text.

E-EDIT

- Self Edit
- Peer Edit
- Professional Edit

INSTRUCTIONS: Use this page to list all of your most common mistakes

SELF EDIT

E-EDIT

- Self Edit
- Peer Edit
- Professional Edit

INSTRUCTIONS: Use this page to list all of your most common mistakes

SELF EDIT

INSTRUCTIONS: Use this page to list the most common mistakes the peer eiditor listed.

PEER

INSTRUCTIONS: Use this page to list the most common mistakes the peer eiditor listed.

PEER

INSTRUCTIONS: List the most common mistakes that were identified by the professional editor. Next, list the mistakes that match the feedback from the professional editor.

Tips:
- **Read your manuscript aloud**
- **Take your time**

PROFESSIONAL

INSTRUCTIONS: List the most common mistakes that were identified by the professional editor. Next, list the mistakes that match the feedback from the professional editor.

Tips:
- **Read your manuscript aloud**
- **Take your time**

PROFESSIONAL

WRITE NOW

WRITE NOW

WRITE NOW

WRITE NOW

SECTION SIX
workbook

NAME IT & FRAME IT

SELECT TITLE AND COVER

Name Your Book:
Give your book a name that will grab your reader and force them to turn it over or flip the pages. Use the following steps to come up with a title to your book.

- Consider what the book's message is, and the essence of its delivery. Explain the message to yourself as if you are learning about it for the first time.
- Use the main character, setting, emotions, or other aspects of the story as the title's center. Using the main character's name, emotions, or the setting can take the reader into the story before opening the book to read it.
- Use social media sites. Create a post that asks for opinions on the titles. Create a poll, a contest, or ask a question. It could also introduce the book and create expectancy among the followers.
- As a last resort, use a title generator online. There are sites created to help authors come up with perfect titles for any book genre.

Give It A Cover:
Framing your book is most important. Having a great title but a cover that isn't eye catching will position your book for failure. Here are a few tips to help create a great book cover design or find a quality designer.

- Find inspiration! Consider the genre of the book is written in and compare it to books in the same genre. What colors, fonts, photos, and typography do they display? Look for bestselling books and take notice of the cover style both the front and the back.
- Decide if the cover will be DIY or if a graphic designer is best. There are inexpensive ways to create a book cover; however, quality is vital. Like a title, the reader will buy the book visually before making an actual purchase. The message is what matters, but the message will remain a mystery to most readers if the cover is not inviting.
- Choose two cover designs and test them out with potential reader. Be open to honest feedback.

NAME IT

BRAINSTORM TITLES

FRAME IT
HOW DO YOU SEE YOUR COVER

WRITE NOW
Resource List

FIVERR

www.fiverr.com

Read reviews, look for seasoned designers, and DO NOT GET THE CHEAPEST OPTION!

REEDSY

www.reedsy.com

Take the time to read and learn about the help they can provide.

UPWORK

www.upwork.com

BOOKBABY

www.bookbaby.com

DIY

CANVA

ADOBE-InDesign/Illustrator

Watch tutorials and practice before you produce and release a product to the public.

WRITE NOW

WRITE NOW

WRITE NOW

WRITE NOW

SECTION SEVEN
workbook

OWN IT & OFFER IT

CHOOSE A PUBLISHING PLATFORM

CHOOSE A PUBLISHING PLATFORM

Where To Begin:

There is more than one route to take when it comes to publishing you book. The great thing is the road to publishing is broad, and the opportunity to get your book before readers is immeasurable if you are willing to do the work. Both non-traditional and traditional publishing exist, and millions of authors have taken both paths. Choose the one that fits your destination and the time you wish to arrive.

Self Publishing:

Self-publishing has been a revolutionary event in the last decade. The gates to publishing have been left open, and companies offer do- it-yourself options with print on demand as a quick way to publish works. Self-publishing with companies such as Amazon, IngramSpark, Lulu gives your book better odds at reaching readers worldwide but at a lower cost.

Traditional Publishing:

Most traditional publishing companies require literary agents as a representative for the manuscript. Submitting a manuscript without an agent will keep you stuck in a well-written book without readers—fortunately, some traditional publishers offer services similar to print-on-demand companies. Choosing that option will allow majority if not complete control of your work.

OWN/OFFER

- Do the research, jot down pros and cons for each company.

Amazon

IngramSpark

Westbow

- Do the research, jot down pros and cons for each company.

Lulu

BookBaby

Barnes & Nobles

- Do the research, jot down pros and cons for each company.

Smashwords

BookBaby

Apple Books

WRITE NOW

WRITE NOW

SECTION EIGHT
workbook

WORK IT & WIN IT

MARKET YOUR BOOK

START YOUR MARKETING

Start Now:
Start marketing now! Please do not make the mistake of waiting until you publish the book to tell people about it. Marketing begins months before your manuscript has made it to the final stage. There are ways to market your book at no cost, low cost, or a big budget. No matter the financial path, start selling your ideas, message, and parts of the story at least 4 to 5 months in advance.

People Need To Know:
People need to know who you are and what you stand for. Your message presented on your social media platforms, word of mouth, podcast, blogs, vlogs, or other social means will build anticipation. Marketing before the book is published will keep your readers ready for what you bring to the platform.

Follow Through & Remain Consistent:
Your readers want to hear from you, so find them and start the conversations. Your ideal person, audience, and reader expect you to give them parts of the whole you will serve later.

Brand Your Name:
An author's name is the author's brand. Ensure every platform is fluid and ties into what your brand or name stands for. Readers should be able to find you, know what you are writing about, and know where to purchase your book. Being fluid is to flow where you should go and never getting stuck in the wrong place. Research to make sure you are using the right platform for your message. Knowing where your ideal audience is will make your book life easier.

WORK IT & WIN IT

WRITE MARKETING CHECKLIST

INSTRUCTIONS: Use the checklist to stay on marketing track.

- [ ] **W** WHERE WILL YOUR AUDIENCE FIND YOU
  SET UP SOCIAL MEDIA SITES/PROFILES
- [ ] **R** RESEARCH AND FIND YOUR RIGHT READERS
  CREATE POST THAT WILL REACH THEM
- [ ] **I** INVEST IN YOURSELF
  GET A WEBSITE OR LANDING PAGE FOR YOU BOOK
- [ ] **T** TARGET YOUR READERS AND CONNECT
  CREATE CONTESTS, EVENTS, PROMOTIONS, PRESALES, ETC
- [ ] **E** EMAIL YOUR READERS, TALK THROUGH EMAIL, BUILD A
  PRODUCTIVE EMAIL LIST

Tip:
Consider hiring someone to help you with marketing.
Invest in yourself, it is important to the life of your book and the deliver of your message.

WRITE NOW
Facebook Marketing

WRITE NOW
Instagram Marketing

WRITE NOW
Linkedin Marketing

WRITE NOW
Youtube Marketing

WRITE NOW
TikTok Marketing

WRITE NOW
PodCast Marketing

WRITE NOW
TV/Radio Marketing

WRITE NOW
Print Marketing

WRITE NOW

TELL YOUR STORY WITHOUT EVER TELLING YOUR BUSINESS

MEET THE AUTHOR

KRISTIE F. GAUTHREAUX

When I wrote my first book, I did not realize I was writing myself out of the trauma I suffered. I was in a same-sex relationship that ended badly with my identity stolen, my vehicle vandalized, my apartment set on fire, and a night in jail for someone I wasn't. It was a very traumatic time in my life, but I chalked it up to be nothing worse than childhood sexual abuse, neglect, and poverty.

Doctors would have easily diagnosed me with PTSD. I lived in fear, suffered from anxiety, had nightmares, and from age five to twenty-four, I had taken on an icy and cruel personality. I formed a shell that no one could penetrate, put on a mask that made every encounter seem like a blissful one until I grew tired of faking, and tore it off. I lived every day in silent stress until God said to me, "Write a book!"

I began writing that book, and it gave me freedom, rest, and a platform to help others. After the first book, I began to gather stressful situations, traumatic events, and mental challenges as they came, and I placed them into a holding cell. While they lie in wait, I would ask God for patience, grace, and wisdom. I would wait on His guidance for a book name and a way with words to put those situations on paper. Though none of my books tell the secrets I have kept, the intent to share my feelings and help others, provided me uncharted liberation. I have been freer in the last fifteen years of my life than I was in the first twenty-five years.

I will spend my life helping others do the same. Put That Shhhh In A Book, PTSB will free many people as it has freed me.

> *"We write our for life, but we also write for the life of others."*

HAVE QUESTIONS?

804 Main Street Ste. A
Baton Rouge, LA 70802
storycoach@kristiegauthreaux.com
www.kristiegauthreaux.com

 @KRISTIEFGAUTHREAUX   KRISTIE F. GAUTHREAUX   WWW.KRISTIEGAUTHREAUX.COM

www.ingramcontent.com/pod-product-compliance
Lightning Source LLC
Chambersburg PA
CBHW041548220426
43665CB00003B/63